Don't Be Afraid
Stories of Christians in Times of Trouble

Rebecca Seiling

Cindy Snider

Illustrations by Manelle Oliphant

A division of Mennonite Publishing Network
Mennonite Church USA and
Mennonite Church Canada

Scottdale, Pennsylvania
Waterloo, Ontario

Don't Be Afraid: Stories of Christians in Times of Trouble
By Rebecca Seiling and Cindy Snider
Illustrations © 2009 by Manelle Oliphant

Copyright © 2009 by Faith & Life Resources, a division of Mennonite Publishing Network, Scottdale, PA 15683 and Waterloo, ON N2L 6H7

All rights reserved. This publication may not be reproduced, stored in a retrieval system, or transmitted in whole or in part, in any form, by any means, electronic, mechanical, photocopying, recording or otherwise without prior permission of Faith & Life Resources.

Faith & Life Resources gratefully acknowledges the financial support of Mennonite Disaster Service for this project. Thanks also to steering committee of Gordon Friesen and Lois Nickel of MDS and Janet Plenert of Mennonite Church Canada, editor Byron Rempel-Burkholder of Faith & Life Resources, and the consulting group from across North America who offered ideas and support for the project.

Unless otherwise noted, Scripture text is quoted, with permission, from the New Revised Standard Version, © 1989, Division of Christian Education of the National Council of Churches of Christ in the United States of America.

International Standard Book Number: 978-0-8361-9478-4
Design by Merrill R. Miller
Printed in USA

Orders and information:
USA: 800-245-7894
Canada: 800-631-6535
www.mpn.net

Contents

Introduction 5

The House That Love Built, by Cindy Snider 7

When Mike's house is destroyed by Hurricane Katrina, his mama Carmen almost gives up hope. But Mike keeps on praying. When Christian strangers come from far away to build a new house, Carmen finds her faith again.

You Are God's Hands, by Cindy Snider 13

Amy accompanies her dad, an international news reporter, when he interviews Nothando, a woman whose life was turned upside down when her husband died. Even though friends and family don't always understand, Nothando has given her life to caring for people in Zimbabwe suffering from AIDS.

No One Will Be Abandoned, by Rebecca Seiling 18

In the year 250, a deadly plague begins spreading throughout the Roman Empire. Bishop Cyprian organizes members of his church to open their homes to sick people abandoned on the streets. Through hard times, the church shows God's love, even for enemies.

Love Behind a Mask, by Rebecca Seiling 25

In the spring of 2003 a strange disease, SARS, threatens to spread in Toronto. As a nurse, Amanda must wear protective clothing at work, and she isn't allowed to eat or sleep with her family. But she knows she is doing what God has called her to do: care for sick people, no matter what.

The Authors 32

Introduction

Do you ever worry that your home might disappear in a storm? Or that you won't have enough to eat? If you get sick, do you ever worry that you won't be able to find a doctor or nurse?

If your life seems pretty safe, you've probably heard stories about trouble coming to other people's lives. You might have seen television shows about a hurricane or a tornado—where people like you and me have lost their homes. Or you might have read about children in Africa who have lost one or both parents to the terrible disease of HIV/AIDS.

Life isn't always safe for everybody. Maybe you've experienced some kind of crisis in your own life. Or maybe you've wondered what would happen if a big disease or a storm came to your part of the country. What would you do? Where would God be?

This book is about people who lived through times of great trouble. Most of us would be afraid if we were in their shoes. And so were they, at first. But then they realized that God's hope shines the brightest when times are tough. Instead of running away from trouble, they reached out with God's love. That is the way God loves us. And because of that, we can be brave and show the same kind of love to others.

No one wishes for tough times. But if our world is shaken up because of a natural disaster or a disease, we can be ready. This book helps us to think about how we and all of God's people can be prepared to live God's love in tough times.

As you read this book, put yourself in the shoes of the people in the stories. To make the experience even more real, do the exercises at the end of each story. As you "think, pray, and act" you will know something about how God can turn bad news around so that hope and love shine bright.

The House That Love Built

My mama sat down in the middle of the street and started crying. The street was full of mud and dirty water and who knows what else. All of a sudden, Mama stood up and turned her face toward the sky. She raised her hands and screamed, "God! How could you let something like this happen to good people like us? Why! Why! Why!"

I was twelve years old—almost a man. I didn't usually cry, but I cried that day. It scared me to see Mama like that. She had always told my sister and me that God would take care of us. I still believed that. I just didn't know how God was going to take care of us this time.

We had always lived in this small town in Mississippi called Pass Christian. You might remember hearing about Hurricane Katrina and how its awesome wind and pounding rain came crashing onto the Gulf Coast of the southern United States. That hurricane was one of the worst natural disasters in the history of our country. It turned our town and our lives upside down.

Here's what happened: Mama, Grandma Eloise, my sister Michelle, and I left Pass Christian on a Sunday morning, the day before Hurricane Katrina was supposed to come ashore. We drove to Jackson, Mississippi, three hours away. My uncles stayed behind. When Mama called them the next day to find out what was happening, they sounded afraid. Then Mama's phone went dead. Nobody could find out what was going on.

The next day Mama and I drove back to Pass Christian. The roads were a mess. Fallen trees and piles of broken stuff were everywhere. When we finally arrived, Mama had to park the car about three miles from our house. We slipped and slid as we walked through the mud and the muck. It smelled so bad that I had to pull my T-shirt up over my nose.

Did you like to play in mud when you were a little kid? Me too, but believe me, you wouldn't want to mess around in this kind of mud! It was slimy and gross. Mama and I kept on walking through it, passing by ruined homes everywhere. The whole town looked like someone had put it in a bag of mud, shook it up, and tossed it back out. It was a mess. The hurricane threw cars, buses, and houses everywhere.

Finally, we came around a corner and saw my uncles. They were alive! After some crying and hugging, we started toward our house. I came to our yard, stopped, and looked all around.

"Mama, where's our house?"

"Mike, it's gone," Mama said, staring straight ahead into the empty space. Her face had that puzzled look that grown-ups get sometimes. We climbed onto a fallen tree to see if we could find anything that looked like our house.

"Mama, look!" I shouted, as I pointed to the middle of the next street. "There's our house!"

We jumped from the tree and ran to the next street. There was a huge hole in the side of our house. Mama tried to unlock all the doors to the house. I thought that was weird since there was a big hole.

Finally I said, "Mama, maybe we can get in here." So we just walked right in. I helped Mama get some clothes. We didn't have time to look for anything else, but Mama said we'd come back with a truck to get all our things.

Then another awful thing happened. A few days later, when we went back to get the rest of our things, we found our home reduced to two piles of rubble, one on each side of the street, left by the bulldozer that had gone down the middle. That's when Mama sat down in the street and cried.

I was in a daze for about a month. Mama wouldn't go back to live in our neighborhood. She sent my sister to live with my aunt in Georgia. Grandma, Mama, and I stayed in Jackson, just waiting and trying to decide what we should do next. I went to a big school that I didn't like. I missed my friends in Pass Christian, and it was hard to make new ones. I missed home even though I knew we didn't have a home anymore.

Every night I asked Mama the same thing. "Have you said your prayers, Mama? God is looking out for us, Mama."

"You pray for me, baby," Mama would say. "I can't pray right now."

Sometimes grownups get discouraged when they have too much on their minds and don't know what to do. They get so overloaded with stress that they can't even pray. At times like that, we kids can help. We can pray when they can't and we can remind them to trust God to make something good come out of the bad.

During that month, I was praying night and day that God would take care of us. And God was listening. Now comes the best part of the story.

Both Grandma and Mama got little travel trailers from the government to live in, so we were able to move back to Pass Christian. Mama started a new job. I thanked God for the good things that were coming back into our lives.

One day, Mama told me, "Mike, I want to get a loan to help us rebuild our lives, but I can't find anyone to help us."

"Have you said your prayers, Mama?" I asked her. "God is looking out for us, Mama."

"You pray for me, baby," Mama sighed. "I can't pray right now."

I smile when I think about what God did next. God gave Mama the idea to write some letters! She wrote to everybody she could

think of who might help us. One day, when she came home from work, she found a note on our door. It was from a group called Samaritan's Purse. They had gotten Mama's letter and were going to find people to rebuild our house. You should have seen the smile on Mama's face when she told me about it!

Week after week volunteers with Mennonite Disaster Service came to work on our new home. Mama offered them money, but they said they didn't want any money. They just wanted to help us.

One day those people even worked in the rain. That's when Mama got back her faith in God. She came home and found a group of people soaking wet, laughing, and getting concrete blocks ready for our house. Mama went right up to those workers and started to cry. She saw God working through the love of the people rebuilding our house. She remembered how much God cares for us.

"These loving people are helping me to trust in God again," Mama told me. "I know now that whatever happens, God is going to fix it."

I used to sneak into the house at night when the workers were gone. Do you know what I found? People's names, Bible verses, and little messages written all over the unpainted walls! It was so cool! I showed them to Mama. She read some of the words out loud. One volunteer had written: "God will not shield you from all trouble, but God will guard you and help you when you face problems. God will always work out his own purposes for you, which is ultimately for your own good."

The names and messages are covered up now so we can't see them. But we remember them and know that we are surrounded by great love in our new home. Mama says that we live in "The House That Love Built."

God kept making good things happen. People from a Baptist church in South Carolina came to help finish the inside of our house. They fixed my basketball goal, too, and even bought a new net for it. They worked all day and prayed in the evening. Lots of those people still come and visit us when they're in our town helping somebody else.

Today, Mama still writes letters, but now it's for people who haven't gotten help yet. She also speaks at lots of events, trying to get help for others. She tells me, "Son, you prayed when I couldn't. You trusted in God's goodness. Thank you for praying every day and for encouraging me. Hard things can happen in life, and when they do, we have to press on and take care of one another."

And that's just what we're doing. We're pressing on, praying, taking care of others, and thanking God every day!

—CS

> **Think:** Think of a time when something scary or bad happened to you. What was your first reaction? Fear? Trust in God? A bit of each?
>
> **Pray:** God, thank you for helping Mike and his family. Thank you that Mike was able to trust in you, even when things were so bad. I want to be able to trust you like that. I want to think of others when times are tough. Amen.
>
> **Act:** With your parents' permission, tape a large piece of poster paper to a wall in your house. Imagine it is like the walls of Mike's new house. Write your name and the names of people you love on your new wall. Write your favorite Bible verses on the wall. Ask your family and friends to add their favorites, too.

Story notes:

This story is based on interviews with Carmen Dedeaux about her family's experience during Hurricane Katrina and its aftermath. A few fictional elements were added, including the telling of the story from Mike's point of view. Thanks to Carmen, her children Michael Jr. (Mike) and Michelle, and their grandmother Eloise Malley, for permission to adapt this story in this way.

You Are God's Hands

My name is Amy Taylor, and I'm eleven. I moved to Zimbabwe, Africa, two years ago, when my dad started a new job as a foreign news correspondent. He interviews people for stories to send back to Canada and the United States. Sometimes I get to go with Dad on his reporting trips.

Africa is a continent, not a country, and it's a lot bigger than I imagined. In fact, it is the second largest of the Earth's seven continents. It is made up of fifty-three countries with around 800 million people. More than a thousand languages are spoken in Africa. It also has lots of animals—like elephants, giraffes, hyenas, lions, monkeys, and warthogs.

But this story isn't about animals, it's about people. It's about a family who lives in Zimbabwe, a country in the southern part of Africa. When my dad interviewed the mother, Nothando,* he let me come along and listen. It was such a touching story that I decided to write it myself. In many ways it's a sad story, but it's also a hopeful story. That's where God comes in.

Nothando is a brave Zimbabwean woman with six children. Last year, when Nothando's husband became ill, she stayed home to take care of him. But in Zimbabwe, Nothando explained, "The men are usually the ones who make money, working at jobs outside the home. So when they are not able to help the family, things get really bad." Because Nothando's husband couldn't earn money, the family ran out of food and they couldn't pay their house payments and utilities. Soon their electricity and water were cut off. The bank took back their house and put it up for sale. Nothando and her children did not know how they were going to survive. Then Nothando had an idea.

"I will take my sick husband to the bank's lawyers so they can see

---

*Nothando (pronounced Noo-tan-doo) is not the woman's real name, but her story is true.

how sick he is and how much we need help," she told her children.

But when they arrived at the law office, the lawyers stopped them at the door and told them to leave. "You must have money to meet with us!" they shouted angrily.

Nothando's husband soon died. Afterward, she also became sick and had to have surgery. Somehow, the family scraped together the money for the treatment. As she spoke, I saw that tears were rolling down Nothando's face. "In our country, women who have no husbands and get sick themselves have no one to care for them. But I was lucky this time."

Nothando paused, because her voice was shaking. I didn't know what to do, so I moved closer to Nothando and held her hand. Dad

told me later that he was very proud of me for reaching out to her. It just seemed like the right thing to do, like something Jesus would do.

Nothando continued, "I thank God for helping me recover quickly from the surgery. But my mind and my body were tired. What was I going to do?"

Nothando thought about all the suffering she and her family had experienced. She began to talk with God about the difficulties that families in Zimbabwe go through when the husbands and fathers get sick or die. "It's especially hard these days," Nothando said, " when there is political turmoil and economic hard times."

There are many diseases and challenges in Africa that are life-threatening, but one of the worst is HIV/AIDS,* which is what Nothando's husband had. HIV/AIDS kills six thousand people every day in Africa—more than wars, famines, and floods. Millions of children have lost both parents to the disease, and now many of them, too, have the virus.

After talking with God about her situation, Nothando realized that God was leading her into a ministry of caring for people with AIDS.

"I received training to care for sick people in my home," she said, "and now I take care of nine people, seven with AIDS and two with cancer. It is hard work. And since we can't always get latex gloves in my country, sometimes I have to use empty plastic sugar bags instead. The rough bags hurt the patients, and they sometimes complain that I no longer care about them."

Nothando smiled. "But God gives me great love for these people. God gives me strength to keep caring for them, even when it is hard. I am God's hands to them." Nothando looked at her hand in mine and smiled at me. Then she took my other hand in hers and said, "And your hands, too, are God's hands."

---

*These stand for *Human Immunodeficiency Virus* (HIV) and *Acquired Immune Deficiency Syndrome* (AIDS). HIV is an illness that spreads from an infected person to others through blood and body fluids, usually through sexual contact or unsterilized needles. Mothers can pass it on to their unborn babies. People usually don't get sick with the virus right away, but when they do, their immune system breaks down and the disease is called AIDS. There is no cure for the virus, but there are medicines that slow down the disease and help people lead fairly normal lives. One reason why so many people around the world are dying of AIDS is that they cannot afford the medicines, or the medicines aren't always available.

Nothando told me that some people believe that we shouldn't help people with AIDS. They think it's always the person's own fault that they are sick. "But who are we to judge?" she asked. "That's up to God. God's job for us is to love and forgive and serve others. That is the example that Jesus gives us. He touched and healed people no matter who might have caused the illness. If it's good enough for Jesus, then it's good enough for me."

Nothando said her family is not always happy about her work because she shares what she has with others, and that leaves less for them. "I am hoping that they also will learn of God's love through my example of helping others," she said. "God gives me that hope. God will give you that hope, too, as you live to serve others."

Nothando lifted both my hands and held them to her face. "You are a good listener," she said. "Now go tell this story to the world. Tell them this story of hope. Tell them this story of God's love."

I looked up at my Dad. "Nothando's right," he said with wink. "I think this is your story to write."

That's how I became a news reporter at age eleven. I wrote this story in Africa and now I'm sharing it with you. Is it a story of hope? Is it a story of God's love? I hope so because that was my assignment.

—CS

Think: Think of a time when doing good might have made you less popular. How did you decide what to do? Nothando decided to help people who were sick, even though it was risky and even though people around her did not always understand. How would you act if you were her?

Pray: God, I don't understand why you allow sickness and suffering in the world. Why don't you do something? People need you! Help me to be your hands of help to others. Amen.

Act: You can help your church donate money or collect items for AIDS Care Kits that Mennonite Central Committee sends to Zimbabwe and other places where AIDS patients need help. For information (including on where your nearest collection center is), go to: www.mcc.org/kits/aids

Story notes:

The true story of Nothando's family was related in a report from Nomusa Chikari, a staff member of Mennonite Central Committee in Bulawayo, Zimbabwe. The narrator, Amy, is fictional, however, as is her visit with Nothando.

No One Will Be Abandoned

Bishop* Cyprian walked the streets of Carthage, praying under his breath, "God, relieve our suffering. Relieve our pain."

As he walked, Bishop Cyprian looked around, shaking his head sadly. Hundreds of people were dying each day, dying alone near the white stone buildings, uncared for because family and friends had deserted them. Dead bodies lay scattered on the cobblestone streets, with no one to claim them or give a proper burial.

Fifty-one-year-old Cyprian was a leader in the church in the North African city of Carthage, the third most important city in the Roman Empire. Born in the year AD 200, he had grown up the son of a wealthy senator. He had the best education possible. But all of this was in the past. At age 46, he became a Christian and gave up his wealth. Two years later, he was appointed as bishop—the leader of all the Christians of Carthage.

Every morning after breakfast, Cyprian walked along the streets of Carthage. Some days he passed by the shores of the Mediterranean Sea and saw the sparkling water as the warm sun shone down on it. Other days, he walked past the luxurious Roman bathhouses in the middle of the city.

Today, in the year 250, he walked by a dark, musty tavern where men sat talking, past the bakery where bread loaves browned in wood-fired brick ovens, past the fountain in the middle of the square where women filled their clay jugs of water for the day. Despite the activity of daily life, there was a heavy sadness that blanketed the city. A deadly plague had spread to Carthage.

Not one family had been spared from fear and grief. From the poorest slaves to the wealthiest Roman officials, everyone knew a

---

*A bishop is the leader of a group of churches.

friend or family member who was sick or who had already died. Carthage was now a city of suffering, sickness, death, and tears. It was a city in constant mourning.

Bishop Cyprian heard a desperate, low moan. Ahead of him, a man lay by the side of a building, coughing and groaning. His bony hands were clutching his chest, his weary eyes squinting at passers-by. He was a young man, possibly the father of young children. But this plague did not spare anyone, not even the young.

Cyprian walked quickly over to the man. "God's peace to you, young man," the bishop said as he bent down and put his hand on the man's shoulder. With his other hand, Cyprian swatted flies from the young man's face.

"Help me," the man said quietly, barely able to speak through his parched, dry lips.

"God is with us in suffering," Cyprian said. "God will not leave you alone." The man opened his eyes a little and slowly lifted his head. His eyes were watery and empty, almost as if he was already dead.

"I have no one to help me. My family is gone, and my friends have left me for dead. How can you say I am not alone?" he asked, then began coughing violently.

The bishop looked the stranger directly in the eyes. "I will help you," Cyprian assured him.

"I am so afraid. What if I die?" asked the man.

"If you die, you will die with dignity, surrounded by people who care about you," the bishop responded. Cyprian took off his outer cloak, and covered the man's body with it. As he got up to leave, Cyprian promised to send help.

The man shook his head. "Why? Why are you doing this? You don't even know me!"

The kind bishop answered, "God knows you and loves you, my son. Rest now. I will get some of my friends, and we will come back for you soon. But please permit me to know your name."

"Donatus," the man said.

Bishop Cyprian walked briskly among the homes in his neighborhood, gathering the people of the church together. The picture of Donatus dying alone on the streets was clear in his mind, and it spurred him on as he knocked on the thick wooden doors of his neighbors. Many women, men, and children followed him to an opening in the street in a curious parade.

He cleared his throat and then spoke earnestly to the group, "My friends, people are dying alone on the streets of our city. It is our duty as followers of Christ to extend our hands to those in need, even if it means risking our own lives. We cannot abandon these people. They must be cared for and loved."

A woman in the crowd was not so sure. "But some of these sick people are the people who have treated us badly because we're Christians. Why should we help them now?"

Bishop Cyprian nodded. "Yes, this is difficult," he said. "What

I am asking you to do is not easy. But there is nothing wonderful about only loving our *own* people. Everyone does that. We must do better. We must extend forgiveness and overcome evil with good by loving those who have persecuted us. God makes the sun rise on us all. So let us do good to all."

After listening to the bishop's speech, a few people were eager to help. But soon, everyone understood that the church needed to help the sick and dying—even people who had been their enemies. What an incredible opportunity they had to be God's light during a dark time. What a blessing to believe that death was not the end for them!

Cyprian continued with his appeal. "We will help people no matter what their background may be. This is what God expects of us. Just this morning I met a young man who needs our help. Who can help to carry him to my home?"

Two young men volunteered to get Donatus. They found him huddled on the street, coughing, with Cyprian's cloak draped around him. They lifted Donatus so that his arms draped over their shoulders and their own strong arms holding his back and his legs. In this way, they carried Donatus to Cyprian's home.

The two men lay Donatus down on a mat that Cyprian had prepared. Cyprian fed Donatus some warm broth, and then he sat near the lonely man as he drifted off to sleep. For Donatus, it was a great relief to have a comfortable place to rest, with someone beside him, caring for him and giving him shelter.

The other people of the church also began to bustle with acts of caring. Young men carried people from the streets to be cared for in homes. Families opened what little space they had in their homes to share it with strangers. An elderly woman made soup, and her granddaughter delivered it. A baker offered fresh loaves of bread. When people died, two women prepared their bodies for burial.

Many of the sick people they found on the streets had been completely abandoned by fearful family members who were afraid of catching the same illness. While others fled in fear, the Christians were inspired by Bishop Cyprian's compassionate words. They courageously sought out sick people and nursed them. Many people still died, but others came back to health. Those who had been sick quickly joined the church's mission to help others in need.

Weeks passed by. One evening, Bishop Cyprian sat at Donatus' bedside. Donatus had been coughing all day. His face was taut, his body thin. The bishop could see that despite his efforts, Donatus was not getting better. Through the open window they could both see the sliver of sun that was setting on the horizon

With a quiet, small voice, Donatus said, "Thank you, Bishop. God has healed my spirit and you've shown me God's love. I'm not afraid to die now."

Bishop Cyprian took the hand of this stranger whom he had befriended on the street. He said, "This is not the end, my friend. It is a new beginning in a place with no pain or crying."

Donatus smiled. He closed his eyes and took in one last, long breath. He breathed out, and then died peacefully.

As weeks and months turned into years, the plague raged on. For 15 long years, the deadly disease claimed the lives of hundreds in Carthage, and thousands throughout the Roman Empire. Although it was a challenge to follow Jesus, the wise bishop knew it was the right way to live. This was a time to show courage and hope in God. Bishop Cyprian told the people, "God will reward you when you give yourselves in service to others."

Surprisingly, the church grew during this terrible time of sickness and death. Other people saw how caring the Christian community was, and they, too became Christians and joined the community. Former enemies became friends and many lives were saved. Hurtful wounds were healed; seeds of forgiveness were planted.

Because Christians cared for each other, many of them survived the deadly plague. Bishop Cyprian and the church in Carthage demonstrated that God's love can heal, and that God is always with us. These Christians showed that selfless love *can* triumph over hatred, sickness and even death.

—RS

Story notes:

This story is based on true historical accounts about Bishop Cyprian and his courageous leadership during the plague of the third century. The rest of the characters are fictional.

Think: Bishop Cyprian organized care for sick people who once hated Christians and treated them badly. How do you relate to your "enemies"? Who could you reach out to in love?

Pray: Where will I see your face, God? In the hungry? In the thirsty? In the stranger at my door? In the sick? In the prisoner?
Open my eyes to see. Open my hands to serve. Show your face to me—just a glimpse—so that I know I'm serving you. Amen.

Act: Some people imagine that God's face looks like all the people's faces mixed together. Find faces in magazines to cut and paste, and cover a piece of poster board with different faces. What does your glimpse of God look like?

Love Behind a Mask

Just before midnight, the phone rang and Amanda awoke from a deep sleep. She squinted at the alarm clock. A call at this hour? She got out of bed and listened to the recorded message. Her heart sank. Slowly, Amanda walked back to bed. She sat down and sighed.

Fear gripped her. Fear that the SARS disease would keep on spreading. Fear for her patients, and for her own family and loved ones.

Amanda's husband Stephen rolled over in bed. "Who was it?" he asked.

"It was Joan, calling from work. Our hospital staff needs to be in quarantine for five days. It's because of SARS. I'll have to stay at home any time I'm not at work. I'll report to work for all of my usual nursing shifts, but I have to come directly home afterward. I can't go for groceries. I can't take the kids to school. They even said I'll have to take a special taxi to work."

Amanda tried to explain all of this calmly. She felt stunned. In her sleepy state, Amanda tried to remember everything Joan had said on the message. This would mean big changes for their family over the next week. Amanda thought of her three children, aged 4, 6, and 8. *How would they react to this news*?

Stephen sat up in bed, now fully awake. "Quarantined? You can't leave the house for five days? Why? You're not sick, are you? Have you been exposed to SARS?"

Amanda reached for his hand. "No, I'm fine," she said, "I *may* have been exposed, but the chance is very slight. They're being extra, extra careful to make sure the disease doesn't keep spreading."

Stephen asked, "So when does the quarantine start?"

Amanda said, "In the morning, the hospital will send me a mask to wear whenever I'm around you and the kids. I can't eat with the family, and I can't share toothpaste, soap, or towels. I'll have to wear gloves when I prepare any food. And I'll have to sleep alone."

Stephen look worried as he continued. "What about the kids? Could you spread it to them?"

"No. I mean, I guess it's *possible* SARS could spread to us, but lots of things are possible. Stephen, we'll be fine. And this quarantine is only for a short while," Amanda reassured him.

Amanda lay back down beside Stephen. He lay awake, staring at the dark ceiling. Amanda tried to go back to sleep, but it was hard. Her troubled mind was racing. *How do I explain this to my three young kids? I know that the work I do is important, but is it so important that I might put my loved ones at risk?* Amanda moved closer to Stephen, embracing him for comfort and assurance.

Amanda is a nurse in a downtown Toronto hospital. Amanda had learned a lot about diseases. She knew that not all diseases lead to death. She knew that just getting up each morning and walking down the street could be a risk. But she refused to live her life in the fear of what *might* happen. Amanda put her trust in God, and took a leap of faith that all would work out. God had called her to be a nurse, and Amanda enjoyed helping patients and their families.

In the spring of 2003, a disease called SARS, or Severe Acute Respiratory Syndrome, had become a medical nightmare in several parts of the world. Within weeks, the deadly virus had spread from one province in China to infect hundreds of people in 37 countries. In Canada, the city most affected was Toronto.

The news had spread quickly, and many people in Toronto were afraid of SARS. Some stayed home from work or kept their children home from school. Some wore masks while outside their homes. News reports showed SARS as being a modern-day plague.

In the early morning, Amanda's oldest child, Adam, woke up first. He was coughing loudly, and his nose was dry and red. Adam slowly walked to his parents' room.

"Hi, Mom," he said, as he burrowed into their bed.

Soon after, Amanda heard the sound of more small feet. Simon and Sarah bounded onto the bed, scrambling for a warm spot in the bed with their parents.

Amanda sat up. With Stephen's help, she explained to her children what was happening. She said, "I have something important to

tell you about my job. What do I do at the hospital?"

Simon was 6 years old. He wore his favorite NHL T-shirt, and his tousled brown hair stuck out in several directions. He confidently answered, "You're a nurse, Mommy. You take care of sick people."

"Right," Amanda said, "and sometimes those people have diseases that make them very, very sick. Right now I'm working with some people who might have a disease called SARS. This disease makes their lungs sick. So, this morning the hospital is going to bring a special mask to the house for me to wear. I'm going to wear a mask for five days so that I don't get sick or make others sick."

Adam asked, "Will other moms be wearing masks too?"

"Other moms and dads who work at hospitals will wear them. We're all going to keep working because patients need to be cared for no matter what disease they have. The masks work really well to keep the bad germs out. I'll work hard to keep all of us healthy."

Amanda hoped that the children would understand what she was telling them about SARS. She didn't want to scare them, but she also didn't want to hide the serious truth from them. She continued. "There are other things that will change for the next while. I have to stay at home when I'm not working. And you kids can't come into my bed in the mornings like you usually do. I have to sleep alone."

Simon sat still, his head lowered. It was hard to know what he was thinking. Sarah said, "Mom isn't sick. But her takes care of sick people. And her takes care of me!" Sarah knew how good it felt to have her mom rub her back and care for her when she felt sick. She hugged her mother, jumped off the bed, and ran to play with her toys.

Adam coughed, this time in a forced way. "I'm sick. Right, Mom?"

Amanda smiled. "Yes, you're still a bit sick, so you can stay home from school today. We don't want people at school to worry when they find out I'm on quarantine. I'll call the school to let them know you'll be absent."

"Do I have SARS?" Adam wondered.

"No, Adam," Amanda laughed. "It's just a regular old cold."

Simon looked at Amanda. "I love you, Mom."

"And I love all of you too. We're going to be just fine. Now let's get dressed and have some breakfast," Amanda instructed.

It was just after breakfast when the doorbell rang. A hospital worker handed Amanda a white N-95 mask. Amanda thanked him, and then sighed as she closed the door. Her quarantine had begun. She stretched the elastic straps over her head to hold the mask in place. The fitted mask covered her mouth and all of her nose. Amanda's fingers tightened the felt-like fabric around her nose. Amanda breathed in and out to make sure it was a tight fit.

The mask worked like a small air purifier. It took in oxygen and filtered out about 95 per cent of the air particles that were 0.3 microns or bigger, like SARS particles.

After childcare was arranged for the day, Stephen went to work. Amanda called for the taxi, and then she rode to the hospital. As soon as she walked in the doors, Amanda put on the SARS gear: a clean new gown, gloves, a mask, and a pair of goggles. Amanda was ready to work.

Amanda performed all of the usual tasks a nurse does every day. She assessed patients' medical conditions, took care of small wounds, and gave people sponge baths to clean them off. If people had air or fluid tubes attached to their bodies, Amanda kept track of them. Much of what Amanda did, however, was to bring comfort and support to the people in her care. She was good at her job, and the patients appreciated her friendly conversation and helpful teaching.

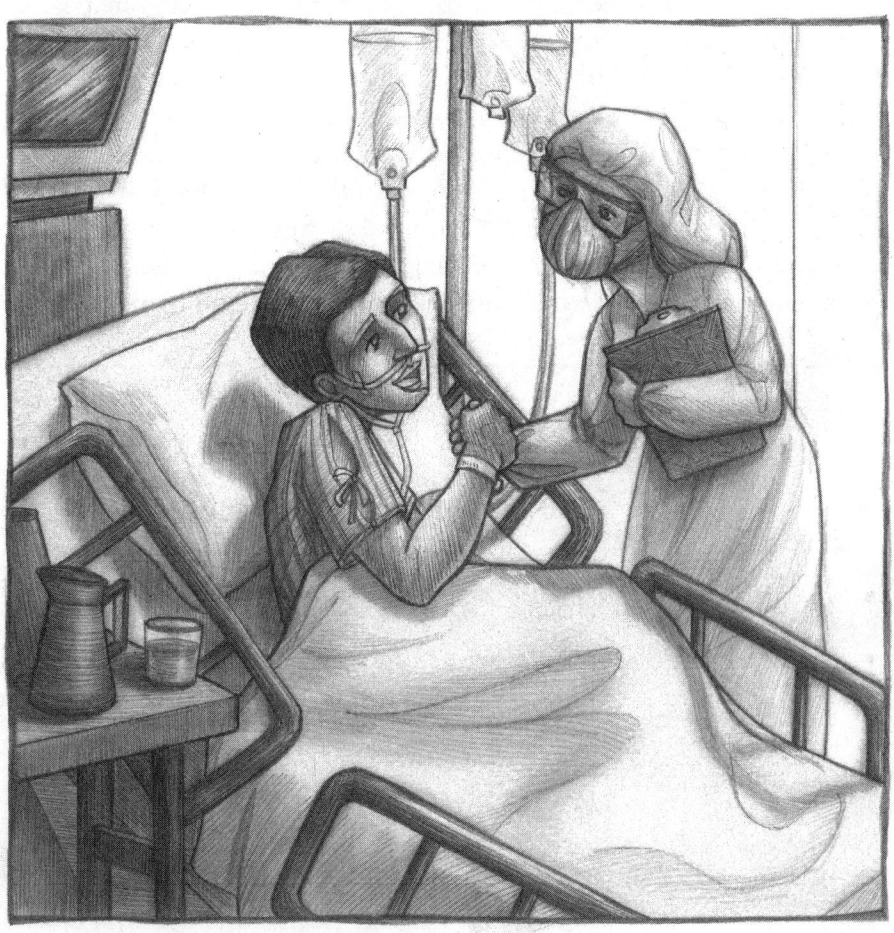

There were risks involved in being a nurse, especially during a time like this. But Amanda knew that if she was careful, taking every extraordinary precaution to prevent spreading germs, her risk of contracting SARS would be very low.

As Amanda made her rounds with the patients, her fear started to melt away. She was doing what she loved to do. This calmed her as she visited with her patients. Her smiling eyes above her mask reassured her patients.

Amanda finished her shift and returned home by taxi. In the early evening, Amanda helped her children with homework. Gradually, the children got used to their masked Mom. Adam joked, "Mom, you could go out for Halloween with that mask!"

When they gathered to eat, the family joined hands. Amanda prayed through her mask, "God, thank you for the courage to work during a time like this. We pray for my patients and their families. Be with them, and give them peace and courage too. Amen."

Amanda took her food to another room, where she took off her mask to eat alone. As she ate, Amanda realized that her fear from the midnight phone call had been replaced with courage. Courage to walk with others, to serve others, and to be willing to take risks. Courage to face fear with confidence that God is with us all along the way.

—RS

Story notes:

This true story is based on interviews with Amanda and on research on the SARS crisis in Toronto in 2003.

Think: Amanda and her family were afraid about the spread of the SARS virus. But their fear seemed to melt away when they took the right precautions and then went ahead and served others. When in your life has fear disappeared when you got involved in caring for others?

Pray: God of boldness, you give us courage. God of light, you give us hope. God of tenderness, you give us love.
God of strength, you give us power. You give us courage to risk, hope to go on, love to embrace others, and power to heal our world. Amen.

Act: Interview someone who works in the medical field, or someone who cares for people who are terminally ill through a hospice program in your community. Ask them what gives them energy and courage in their work.

The Authors

Rebecca Seiling is the author of *Plant a Seed of Peace* (Herald Press), a book of stories about peace heroes. She has written and edited for the *Gather 'Round* Sunday school curriculum and has taught elementary and high school. Rebecca lives in Waterloo, Ontario, with her husband and two daughters. She attends St. Jacobs Mennonite Church, and loves to travel, garden, and read.

Cindy Snider is a freelance writer and the author of *Finding Anna Bee* (Herald Press), a children's novel. She lives with her two dogs in Wichita, Kansas, and is a member of Mennonite Church of the Servant in Wichita, Kansas. Besides writing, she loves to travel with her nieces and nephews.

The illustrator
Manelle Oliphant is an illustrator from West Valley, Utah. Her work appears in a variety of books, magazines and other media.